EASY
TO
MAKE
RECIPES
for
Beginners

SALMON

Index

Cover pictures *front:* "Dinnertime" *by George Hardy*
back: "The Sweet Shop" *by Harry Brooker*
Title page: "Shelling Peas" *by Carlton Smith RI*

Printed and Published by J. Salmon Ltd., Sevenoaks, England © Copyright

LEARNING TO COOK is a useful and practical skill which everyone should try to acquire; it is also very satisfying to be able to produce simple and tasty dishes for oneself and one's family and friends.

There are some essential safety rules to remember before starting to cook and young people should take special care, especially if they are short and cannot easily reach the stove; ask grown-ups to help if necessary.

In the kitchen some things can be dangerous, as for example gas burners, hot plates and ovens, sharp knives, hot water and steam which can easily scald you. Hot saucepans are potentially dangerous; they can be tipped over on the stove so always make sure that the handles are turned away from the burners and the pan is sitting firmly on the top of the stove.

Remember to put on an apron before you begin, to protect your own clothes and, more importantly, to prevent dust and hairs off you getting into the food. Also, if you have long hair, tie it back and avoid wearing loose clothes which could catch in hot pans. Roll up your sleeves before you begin.

Make sure you assemble all the equipment and ingredients you will need for a recipe, before you start work.

Always use oven gloves when handling hot dishes and pans, particularly when putting them into or taking them out of the oven. Do not use woollen or other ordinary gloves. Cleanliness is most important – before you begin to prepare food, always **WASH YOUR HANDS** thoroughly to make sure they are clean and scrub your nails. Also, if you have handled raw meat, wash your hands again and your utensils before doing anything further. Another thing to remember is to use different chopping boards for meat and vegetables, or wash the board very thoroughly between uses.

Finally, **BE SENSIBLE**, have a go and enjoy yourself!

SOME USEFUL TIPS

GREASING and LINING To grease a cake tin, a pudding basin or a baking sheet to prevent the product sticking when you try to turn it out, it is necessary to smear a thin layer of butter or margarine on all the inside surfaces. In some cases further treatment is necessary to prevent sticking. This is called "greasing and lining" which means first the inside is to be coated as stated. Then you will need to cut out with scissors a piece or pieces of greaseproof paper to fit the base and/or the inside of the tin, and then stick this paper to the butter or margarine coating.

RUBBING IN Some recipes require you to "rub in the fat". This means that it is necessary to rub and squeeze the fat and flour in the mixing bowl between your thumbs and fingers repeatedly, until all the fat has been absorbed into the flour. When this is complete the resulting mixture will achieve a crumbly texture which is said to resemble fresh breadcrumbs.

BEATING Where the recipe requires you to "beat" the mixture, steady the mixing bowl firmly with your free hand and, using a wooden spoon in the other hand, **STIR ENERGETICALLY** with a rotary movement of the wrist, lifting the mixture as you go to get as much air into it as possible.

MEASURING Always measure ingredients carefully. Use either Imperial or Metric measurements, one or the other, but do not mix the two in the same recipe.

Peppermint Creams

Nothing to do but mix together, roll out and cut into circles.

1 lb (450g) icing sugar
4 tablespoons condensed milk
A few drops of oil of peppermint

Required: **A mixing bowl, a sieve and a rolling pin.**

First carefully sieve the icing sugar into the bowl, and then gradually mix in the condensed milk to form a stiff paste. Next, add the peppermint oil and work the mixture with the hands until the flavouring is evenly distributed. Dust a pastry board or work surface with icing sugar, turn out the mixture on to it and roll it to about ¼ inch (6cm) thick with a rolling pin dusted with sugar. Alternatively put between 2 layers of non-stick paper and roll out. Now stamp out into small rounds (size according to preference) with a plain cutter, or use for example an inverted sherry glass. Re-roll the remaining mixture until it is all used up. Place the mints on a tray or dish and leave in a cool place to dry out.

Iced Party Biscuits

Crisp, thin shortbread-type biscuits; very more-ish.

**2 oz (50g) plain flour   1 oz (25g) ground rice   1 oz (25g) caster sugar
2 oz (50g) soft margarine**

ICING
1 oz (25g) icing sugar   Water

***Required:* A mixing bowl, a rolling pin, a 2 inch (5cm) pastry cutter,
a baking sheet and a wire rack.**

Preheat the oven to 350°F (180°C) or Mark 4. Grease the baking sheet. Put all the ingredients into the bowl and mix together with the hands to produce a pastry dough. Roll out the dough on a floured surface to barely ¼ inch (5mm) thick and cut out rounds with a pastry cutter, re-rolling the dough until it is all used up. Put the biscuits on the baking sheet and prick each one all over with a fork. Bake in the oven for about 12 to 15 minutes until the biscuits are a pale brown. Transfer them to a wire rack to cool.

To make the icing, put the icing sugar into a cup and gradually mix in only just a very little cold water to form a stiff paste. Add a drop of food colouring to the icing, if preferred, or make some white and some coloured. Finally, put a blob of icing in the centre of each biscuit when they are cold. Makes about 8 biscuits.

Simple Shortbread

A quick and easy-to-make teatime treat.

4 oz (110g) butter
3 oz (75g) sugar
6 oz (150g) self-raising flour

Required: **A saucepan and a 6½ to 7 inch (16 to 18cm) sandwich tin.**

Preheat the oven to 350°F (180°C) or Mark 4. Grease the cake tin. First put the butter and sugar in the saucepan and melt very gently over a low heat. When melted, remove from the heat, add the flour and mix well together. Put the mixture into the tin and press down evenly with the fingers. Bake in the oven for about 15 to 20 minutes until the shortbread is light golden brown. When cooked, mark into segments with a sharp knife and leave in the tin to get cold. When cold, cut through the segments and turn out. Makes 8 biscuits.

"The Sore Foot" by C. Pattein

Chicken and Egg Toasts

A simple supper dish based on scrambled eggs.

**4-6 oz (110-175g) cooked chicken, finely chopped
4 rashers streaky bacon   1½ oz (40g) butter
4 large eggs   1 tablespoon milk   Salt and pepper
Slices of hot buttered toast
Chopped fresh parsley to garnish**

***Required:* A mixing bowl and a saucepan.**

Preheat the grill. First cut off the rind from the the bacon rashers, then form them into neat rolls and grill them until they are nice and crisp and brown. Put them aside and keep warm. Break the eggs into the bowl, add the milk, season with salt and pepper and beat well. Add the chopped chicken pieces. Melt the butter in the saucepan over a low heat, pour in the chicken/egg mixture and scramble, scraping the curds gently from the bottom of the pan with a spoon, until lightly set. Meanwhile, make the slices of toast and butter liberally while still warm. Pile helpings of scrambled egg on each slice, top with the warm bacon rolls and garnish with chopped parsley. Serves 4.

Victoria Sponge Cake

The classic English sponge made by the easy "all-in-one" method.

6 oz (175g) soft margarine   6 oz (175g) caster sugar
6 oz (175g) self-raising flour   1 rounded teaspoon baking powder
3 large eggs
4 tablespoons raspberry jam
Extra caster sugar for dusting

Required: **A mixing bowl, two 7 inch (18cm) sandwich tins and a wire rack.**

Preheat the oven to 375°F (190°C) or Mark 5. First grease the tins and line the bases with greaseproof paper. Measure the margarine, sugar, flour and baking powder into the bowl, break in the eggs and beat well together for 2 minutes until the mixture is smooth and well blended. Next, divide the mixture equally between the 2 tins and smooth out. Bake in the oven for about 20 minutes until well risen, golden brown on top and springy to the touch. Turn out on to a wire rack, peel off the paper and leave to cool. When cool, spread the flat side of one cake with a good layer of raspberry jam, lay the flat side of the other cake on top and, finally, dust the top of the cake with caster sugar.

Strawberry Cream Dessert

Perfect as a summer treat; just strawberries, cream and gelatine.

1 lb (450g) ripe strawberries
6 oz (175g) caster sugar
1 pint (570ml) double cream, lightly whipped
1½ oz (40g) gelatine   5 fl.oz (150ml) hot water

Required: **2 bowls, a sieve and 6 sundae glasses.**

First put the strawberries into a bowl and mash to a pulp with a fork; then stir in the sugar. Rub the mixture through a sieve into the bowl and then fold in the lightly whipped cream. Put the gelatine into another bowl, add the hot water and let it dissolve. Set aside to allow it to cool and then mix it gently into the fruit/ cream mixture and keep stirring until it begins to set. Then pour the mixture into the individual sundae glasses (or if preferred into a jelly mould) and leave to set completely before serving. If in a mould, stand the mould in hot water for a few seconds to loosen before turning out and serving. Serves 6.

Smoked Haddock Charlotte

Tasty smoked fish and bread-and-butter make up this simple baked dish.

1 lb (450g) smoked haddock   1 egg, beaten
5 fl oz (150ml) milk   Grated rind of ½ lemon
1 tablespoon chopped fresh parsley   Salt and pepper
5 slices white bread, buttered, with crusts removed and cut into fingers

Required: **A mixing bowl and a medium-size pie dish.**

Preheat the oven to 350°F (180°C) or Mark 4. First, separate the haddock flesh from the skin and remove all the bones. Then mince the fish or cut it into small pieces, put it into the bowl with the beaten egg, milk, lemon rind and parsley, season with salt and pepper to taste, and mix all well together. Next, line the bottom and side of the pie dish with about half of the bread slices, butter side outwards. Now put a layer of half of the fish mixture on the bread in the pie dish and cover with a layer of bread-and-butter. Repeat, putting in another layer of fish and finish with a final layer of bread-and-butter, butter side upwards. Bake in the oven for 40 to 45 minutes until the top is crisp and golden brown. Serves 4. Un-smoked haddock can be used if preferred, but smoked fish has more flavour.

Cheese Fritters

Tasty, cheesey batter fried to make an easy supper dish.

**7 fl oz (200ml) double cream   2 oz (50g) flour   4 eggs
4 oz (110g) Cheddar cheese, grated   2 oz (50g) butter
Freshly grated nutmeg   Pinch ground mace (optional)
1 teaspoon salt   1 teaspoon pepper   Oil for frying**

Required: **A small saucepan, a mixing bowl, a balloon whisk, a frying pan
and kitchen paper.**

First put the cream into the saucepan and whisk in the flour. Put the pan on the heat, bring the mixture to the boil, whisking all the time, then remove the pan from the heat and set aside to cool. Next, break the eggs into the mixing bowl, whisk them until they are light and frothy, and then beat them into the cooled cream in the saucepan. Stir in the grated cheese and all the remaining ingredients and beat the batter until well mixed together. Now heat a little oil in a frying pan until it is really hot, drop in tablespoons of the batter and fry them for about 1 minute on each side until they are golden and puffy. When cooked, transfer the fritters to drain on kitchen paper on a warm plate and eat while still hot. Serves 4.

Oatmeal Crunch

Easier to make than flapjack. Just melt, mix and press into the tin.

4 oz (110g) hard margarine
3 oz (75g) Demerara sugar
5 oz (150g) porridge oats

Required: **A mixing bowl, a saucepan and a 7 inch (18cm) round sandwich tin.**

First well grease the tin. Put the margarine and sugar into the saucepan and melt very gently over a low heat, stirring occasionally. When they are just melted, take the pan off the heat, add the oats and mix together until all is well blended. Finally, put the mixture into the tin, spread it out evenly and press down firmly with the fingers. Bake in the oven for about 15 minutes until it is golden brown and crunchy. Remove the tin from the oven and, while still warm, cut the flapjack into wedges with a sharp knife, but leave in the tin to get cold before finally turning out.

"The Knitting Lesson" by Carlton Smith RI

Corned Beef & Baked Bean Hash

Everybody likes corned beef and baked beans. A quick and easy meal to prepare.

1 lb (450g) potatoes
1 tablespoon olive oil
1 oz (25g) butter
1 onion, peeled and chopped
200g can corned beef, diced
200g can baked beans
Worcestershire sauce

Required: **A saucepan and a frying pan.**

First peel the potatoes and cook in salted water until nearly tender. Remove from the heat, drain and allow to cool. When cool, cut them into small cubes. Now heat the oil and butter in the frying pan and gently fry the chopped onion until soft, but not brown. Then add the diced potato to the onion in the pan, increase the heat and continue frying until the potatoes are browned. Add the diced corned beef and the baked beans with a good dash of Worcestershire sauce, stir well, turn down the heat and continue cooking on the stove to heat through thoroughly. When everything is hot the dish is ready. Serve direct from the pan with crusty bread. Serves 2 to 3.

Savoury Pinwheels

A tasty, Marmite flavoured party snack, or for nibbling at any time.

8 oz (225g) prepared shortcrust pastry
4 teaspoons Marmite
3 oz (75g) Cheddar cheese, grated

Required: **A mixing bowl, a rolling pin, a grater, a baking sheet and a wire rack.**

Preheat the oven to 400°F (200°C) or Mark 6. First grease the baking sheet. Then roll out the pastry thinly on a floured surface to a rectangle about 8 x 10 inches (20 x 25cm) and neatly trim the edges. Now spread the Marmite evenly all over the pastry to within ½ inch (1cm) of the edges and sprinkle over the grated cheese. Next, roll up the pastry from a long edge so that it is like a Swiss Roll, dampen the back edge with a little water to seal, and then trim off the ends. Cut into slices about ¼ inch (5mm) thick with a sharp knife and arrange the slices on their sides on the baking sheet. Bake in the oven for about 10 to 15 minutes until the slices are bubbling. Remove from the oven and transfer to a wire rack to cool.

Chocolate Truffles

Soft chocolate balls rolled in desiccated coconut.

4 oz (110g) plain block chocolate (best quality)
2 oz (50g) icing sugar
1½ tablespoons unsweetened evaporated milk
½ teaspoon vanilla essence
Desiccated coconut

Required: **A small basin and a small saucepan**

First, half-fill the saucepan with water and bring it nearly to the boil. Meanwhile break up the chocolate into small pieces and put into the basin. Now set the basin over the pan of hot but not boiling water to melt the chocolate. When melted, remove the basin from the pan, stir in the icing sugar, evaporated milk and vanilla essence and blend well together. No cooking is required, so next take teaspoonsful of the mixture and roll in the hands to shape into small balls. Put a quantity of desiccated coconut on to a plate and now roll in it each chocolate ball so that it is coated all over. These truffles can be kept in an airtight tin in the refrigerator for up to 3 days.

"Ill prepared" by G. B. O'Neill

Cheese and Potato Bake

These baked, cheesey potatoes can be eaten on their own or as part of a larger meal.

6 medium potatoes, peeled and cut into thin slices
2-4 oz (50-110g) butter
2 medium onions, peeled and thinly sliced   2 cloves garlic, peeled and crushed
4 oz (110g) Cheddar cheese, grated
1 pint (570ml) full cream milk
Salt and pepper

Required: **A shallow ovenproof dish and kitchen foil.**

Preset the oven to 325ºF (170ºC) or Mark 3. First grease the dish and arrange a layer of potato slices over the base. Dot with little lumps of butter, sprinkle with salt and black pepper, add a layer of onion with a little crushed garlic and then spread over about one quarter of the grated cheese. Continue making layers like this, and finish with a layer of cheese over a top layer of potatoes. Pour on the milk, cover the dish with kitchen foil and seal round the edges. Cook in the oven for 1½ hours then remove the foil and continue cooking for about a further 30 minutes until the potatoes are tender. This makes an excellent light supper dish, served on its own or it is a good accompaniment to many meat dishes.

Apple & Bramble Crumble

Stewed fruit with a crunchy, crumbly topping.

1 lb (450g) cooking apples, peeled, cored and sliced
8 oz (225g) blackberries, washed and drained
4-6 oz (110-175g) granulated sugar, according to taste

CRUMBLE

4 oz (110g) flour   2 oz (50g) porridge oats   Pinch of salt
4 oz (110g) butter or margarine   4 oz (110g) Demerara sugar

Required: **A large pie dish and a mixing bowl.**

Preheat the oven to 375°F (190°C) or Mark 5. First mix together the apple slices and blackberries and put into the pie dish. Add enough sugar according to taste and just a very little water. For the crumble topping, put the flour, oats, salt and butter or margarine into the mixing bowl and work in the fat by rubbing the mixture between the fingertips and thumbs until it resembles fresh breadcrumbs. Now stir in the Demerara sugar and then sprinkle the crumble mixture all over the fruit in the dish. Bake in the oven for about 15 minutes, then reduce the oven temperature to 350°F (180°C) or Mark 4 and continue baking for about a further 35 to 40 minutes until the top is browned. Serves 4.

Marshmallow Crunchies

No cooking required: just melt in a pan and mix together.

4 oz (110g) marshmallows
4 oz (110g) slab toffee or wrapped toffees
4 oz (110g) butter
Rice Crispies

Required: **A saucepan and greaseproof paper.**

First put the marshmallows, toffee (unwrap if they are wrapped) and butter into the pan and melt very slowly over a gentle heat, stirring all the time. When melted, remove the pan from the heat and stir in just enough Rice Crispies to make a stiff mixture. Then, using a teaspoon, drop lumps of the mixture about the size of a walnut on to the greaseproof paper and leave to cool and harden. When cool store in an airtight container.

"A Bowl of Cherries" by Joseph Clark

Vegetable Macaroni Cheese

The vegetables make this more of a meal than plain macaroni cheese.

6 oz (175g) macaroni   8 oz (225g) carrots, finely sliced
8 oz (225g) courgettes, finely sliced   2 inner celery sticks, finely sliced
½ pint (2 cups) vegetable stock (use a stock cube)   ½ pint (2 cups) milk approx.
1½ oz (40g) butter   2 oz (50g) flour   Salt and pepper
4 oz (110g) hard mature Cheddar cheese, grated

Required: **2 saucepans, a colander, a large frying pan and a large ovenproof dish.**

Cook the macaroni in a pan of boiling salted water until just tender (about 15 minutes). Meanwhile, put all the sliced vegetables into a saucepan with the stock (use a stock cube dissolved in hot water), bring to the boil and simmer for 5 to 10 minutes (how long will depend on how thinly the vegetables are sliced) until they are tender but still a little crisp. Drain the vegetables over a bowl and keep the stock. Add sufficient milk to the stock to make it up to 1 pint (570ml). Melt the butter in the frying pan, stir in the flour and cook for 1 minute over a low heat. Next, stir in the stock and cook for another minute or two to thicken. Take the pan off the heat, stir in about ¾ of the cheese and season. Drain the macaroni and add with the vegetable mixture to the stock mixture, stir, and spoon it into the dish. Sprinkle the rest of the cheese over the top and cook under a hot grill until lightly browned on top. Serves 4.

Rice Pudding

Just mix the ingredients and cook slowly. So easy and an old family favourite.

2 oz (50g) pudding rice
1 pint (570ml) full cream milk
1 oz (25g) caster sugar
½ oz (15g) butter
A nutmeg to grate

Required: **A mixing bowl, a sieve and a 1 pint (570ml) ovenproof dish**

Preheat the oven to 350ºF (180ºF) or Mark 4. First grease the dish. Next wash the rice in a sieve under running water to clean and remove excess starch, and drain well. Put the drained rice into the ovenproof dish, add the sugar and butter and pour in the milk. Cook in the oven for about 25 to 30 minutes until a pale golden skin has formed. Remove from the oven, stir in the skin and grate some nutmeg over the top of the dish. Lower the oven temperature to 275ºF (140ºC) or Mark 1. Return the dish to the oven and cook for a further 1½ to 2 hours until the rice is cooked. Serve just as it is or with single cream. Serves 4.

Plain Scones

Delicious eaten buttered or with jam and clotted cream.

8 oz (225g) self-raising flour
1 level teaspoon baking powder
2 oz (50g) butter (not straight from the fridge)
1 oz (25g) caster sugar
7 tablespoons milk

Required: **A mixing bowl, a rolling pin, a 2½ inch (6 cm) pastry cutter, a baking sheet and a wire rack.**

Preheat the oven to 425°F (220°C) or Mark 7. Grease and lightly flour the baking sheet. First put the flour and baking powder into the bowl then rub in the butter with the fingers until the mixture resembles breadcrumbs. Add the sugar and the milk and mix to a soft dough. Roll out the dough on a floured surface to ½ inch (1cm) thick and cut out rounds with a pastry cutter, re-rolling the dough until it is all used up. Put the scones on the baking sheet and brush the top of each one with a little milk. Bake in the oven for about 12 to 15 minutes until golden brown on top and the scone sounds hollow when the base is tapped. When cooked, transfer to a wire rack to cool. Makes about 8 scones.

Bacon & Egg Pie

Made like a flan with a pastry topping. A tasty supper dish.

1 lb (450g) ready-made shortcrust pastry
2 pork sausages   3 rashers bacon, streaky or back, de-rinded
2 eggs
Some fresh chopped parsley   Salt and pepper

Required: **An 8inch (20cm) round sponge cake tin, a mixing bowl and a rolling pin.**

Preheat the oven to 400°F (200°C) or Mark 6. First grease the cake tin. Roll out half of the pastry on a floured surface and use it to line the cake tin. Trim the edge. Now cut up the sausages into small chunks and the bacon into pieces and spread them out evenly in the pastry case. Break the eggs into the bowl, beat them together and pour them over the meat. Sprinkle over the chopped parsley and season with salt and pepper. Roll out the remaining pastry, damp the edge of the pastry in the tin, cover the pie, seal the edge firmly using a fork to press down, and trim with a knife. Bake in the oven for about 45 minutes until the pastry is golden brown. Serve cold with a salad. Serves 3 to 4.

Easy-mix Fruit Cake

Fruit cakes are always popular. This easy recipe uses the "all-in-one" method.

6 oz (175g) soft margarine
6 oz (175g) granulated sugar
2 oz (50g) self-raising flour   6 oz (175g) plain flour
1 teaspoon ground mixed spice   10 oz (275g) mixed dried fruit
2 oz (50g) glacé cherries, halved
2 eggs   1 tablespoon milk
Pinch of salt   Grated zest of 1 orange (optional)

Required: **A mixing bowl and a 2 lb loaf tin.**

Preheat the oven to 325°F (170°C) or Mark 3. First grease and line the tin with greaseproof paper. Put all the ingredients (except the eggs) into the bowl. Then break in the eggs, add the milk and mix thoroughly with a wooden spoon until well blended together. Finally, put the mixture into the tin, spread it out roughly and bake for 1 to 1½ hours or until a skewer pushed into the cake comes out clean, without any mixture sticking to it. Leave the cake in the tin to cool before turning it out.

Sausage Stew

A substantial meal with lots of flavour.

**2 lbs (900g) pork sausages   2 tablespoons cooking oil   1 medium onion, chopped
2 cloves garlic, chopped   Large tin of chopped tomatoes   1 tablespoon tomato purée
½-1 teaspoon dried mixed herbs   1 teaspoon sugar   1 dessertspoon cornflour
Salt and pepper   ½ pint vegetable stock (use a stock cube)
2 cups frozen peas**

Required: **A large saucepan and a mixing bowl.**

First, cut the sausages in half. Heat 1 tablespoon of oil in the saucepan and fry the sausages slowly until browned; then remove them from the pan and set aside. Add another tablespoon of oil to the pan and fry the chopped onion and garlic until soft but not brown. Replace the sausages in the pan and add the chopped tomatoes, tomato purée, herbs and sugar, and stir. Mix the cornflour with a tablespoon of stock in a bowl, then stir in the remaining stock (use a stock cube dissolved in hot water) and mix well. Add the stock to the pan, stir and season well with salt and pepper. Bring to the boil, lower the heat, put a lid on the pan and simmer for 35 to 40 minutes, adding more boiling water during cooking, if required. Add the peas 5 minutes before the end of the cooking time. Serves 4 to 6.

"The Little Water Carriers" by P. E. Frere

Banana Milk Shake

A simple ice-cream drink for a hot day.

2 bananas
2 scoops vanilla ice-cream
1 tablespoon light soft brown sugar
1 pint (570ml) milk

***Required:* A mixing bowl and a balloon whisk.**

First peel the bananas, put them into the bowl with the ice-cream and mash well together with a fork. Now add the sugar and beat the mixture until it is creamy. Next add the milk and whisk until the mixture is light and frothy. Pour the milk shake into a jug and serve in long glasses with ice cubes or a scoop of ice cream.

Lemon Surprise

A delicious, tangy lemon-flavoured mousse.

1 large tin condensed milk
1 small tin sterilised cream
Juice of 2 large lemons
Whipped cream and glacé cherries to decorate

Required: **A mixing bowl and a pretty glass serving bowl.**

Put the condensed milk and the cream into the mixing bowl and mix well together. Add the lemon juice a little at a time, beating well after each addition, until the mixture thickens and no longer tastes of condensed milk. Transfer the mixture, which is now a mousse, into the serving bowl and put into the refrigerator to set and keep until it is required. Before serving, decorate the top of the mousse with blobs or whorls of whipped cream and with glacé cherries. Serves 6.

Cottage Pie

Minced beef is the foundation of this universally popular meal.

**1 lb (450g) minced beef   1 large onion, chopped   1 large carrot, chopped small
1 tablespoon flour   ½ teaspoon ground cinnamon   ½ teaspoon dried mixed herbs
1 tablespoon tomato purée   ½ pint (275ml) beef stock (made with a stock cube)
Salt and pepper   Oil for frying
1½ - 2 lb (700-900g) potatoes, peeled   1 oz (25g) butter**

***Required:* A saucepan, a frying pan and an ovenproof dish.**

First put the potatoes on to boil in a pan of salted water. Remove from the heat when cooked. Preheat the oven to 400°F (200°C) or Mark 6. Grease the ovenproof dish. First fry the onions in a little oil until they are soft but not brown then add the meat and carrot to the pan and fry for about 4 to 5 minutes, stirring occasionally, until the meat is browned. Now add the flour, cinnamon, mixed herbs and tomato purée, stir in the hot stock (use a stock cube dissolved in hot water), bring back to simmering and cook for a further 20 minutes. Meanwhile drain and mash the potatoes and stir in the butter. Put the meat mixture into the dish, cover with the mashed potato and spread out evenly with a fork. Bake in the oven for about 25 to 30 minutes until nicely browned on top. Serves 4.

Leek & Potato Soup

Soup is so easy to make and is such a useful standby meal in itself.

**1 lb (450g) leeks, washed and sliced thinly   1 lb (450g) potatoes, peeled and diced
2 onions, peeled and sliced thinly   2 oz (50g) butter   2 oz (50g) flour
2 pints (1150 ml) chicken stock (use stock cubes)   Pinch of ground nutmeg
Pinch of dried thyme   Salt and pepper   3 tablespoons single cream
Chopped fresh parsley to garnish**

Required: **A large saucepan and a food processor (or a potato masher).**

First melt the butter in the large saucepan, then add all the sliced vegetables, stir well together with a wooden spoon to coat with butter and cook them for 10 to 15 minutes until they are softened, but not brown. Stir in the flour and then gradually stir in the stock (use stock cubes dissolved in hot water). Add the nutmeg and thyme and season with salt and pepper. Bring to the boil, lower the heat, put a lid on the pan and simmer for about 20 to 30 minutes until the vegetables are really soft. When ready, purée the mixture in a processor or blender (or if not available, use a potato masher). Return the soup to a clean saucepan, check the seasoning and heat through to serve, garnished with parsley; or serve chilled. Serves 6.

Chocolate Coconut Fingers

Iced cake slices made with coconut and cocoa powder.

4 oz (110g) hard margarine   2 oz (50g) granulated sugar   4 oz (110g) self-raising flour
2 oz (50g) desiccated coconut   2 teaspoons cocoa powder

ICING
4 oz (110g) icing sugar   1 teaspoon cocoa powder   Water to mix

Required: **A small saucepan, a mixing bowl and a 7 inch (18mm) square, shallow tin.**

Preheat the oven to 350°F (180°) or Mark 4. Grease the tin. First, put the margarine and sugar into the saucepan and melt over a gentle heat until all the sugar is dissolved. Take the pan off the heat and stir into the mixture the flour, coconut and cocoa powder. Mix thoroughly. Put the mixture into the tin, spread it out and press it down gently with the fingers. Bake in the oven for 15 to 20 minutes until risen and golden brown. Meanwhile, make the icing; put the icing sugar and cocoa powder into the bowl and mix together with a very little water; only just enough to make a stiff icing. When the cake base is cooked, ice the top immediately, using a knife warmed in hot water to spread out. When the icing has set, and while the cake is still just warm, cut it into fingers in the tin before turning out.

Baked Custard

An favourite old-fashioned pudding which is so easy to make.

1 pint (570ml) milk
3 eggs
1 oz (25g) caster sugar
A nutmeg for grating

Required: **A mixing bowl, a saucepan, a strainer, a grater and a large pie dish.**

Preheat the oven to 275°F (140°C) or Mark 1. Grease the pie dish with butter. First break the eggs into the mixing bowl and beat together. Then put the milk into the saucepan and heat gently but **DO NOT** boil. When hot, pour the milk slowly over the beaten eggs, stirring all the time, and then stir in the sugar. Strain the mixture into the pie dish and grate nutmeg all over the top. Put into the oven and bake for about 1 hour until set and lightly browned on top. Serves 4.

Cheesey Fish Pie

This simple fish pie makes a substantial meal.

**1½ lb (700g) potatoes, peeled   1 lb (450g) white fish (cod or haddock)
½ pint (275ml) each of milk and water, mixed   4 slices of lemon
Chopped fresh parsley   Salt and pepper   4 oz (110g) Cheddar cheese, grated**

Required: **A saucepan, a large frying pan, a grater and an ovenproof dish.**

First peel the potatoes and boil them in a pan of salted water. When cooked, drain and mash with a little butter and milk and leave in the saucepan. Meanwhile, pour the milk/water mix into the frying pan, add the fish, the slices of lemon and a good pinch each of chopped parsley, salt and pepper. Set the pan over the heat on the stove, bring to the boil and then simmer gently for about 5 to 8 minutes until the fish is cooked. Remove the fish from the pan, flake the flesh and remove any skin and bone. Add the flaked fish to the mashed potato with half the grated cheese and then add some of the milk/water stock, sufficient to moisten the mixture. Return the pan to the stove and then heat gently, stirring all the time until the mixture is hot. When hot, spoon the mixture into the ovenproof dish, spread out and sprinkle the remaining grated cheese over the top. Heat the grill, and finish the pie under a hot grill until the top is lightly browned. Serves 4.

Rock Cakes

So simple to make; just mix together and bake.

8 oz (225g) plain flour   1 teaspoon baking powder
3 oz (75g) butter (not straight from the fridge)
2 oz (50g) caster sugar
4 oz (110g) currants
½ teaspoon ground mixed spice
1 egg, beaten   3 tablespoons milk

Required: **A mixing bowl, a baking sheet and a wire rack.**

Preheat the oven to 400°F (200°C) or Mark 6. Grease the baking sheet. First put the flour and baking powder into the bowl and rub in the butter with the fingers until the mixture resembles breadcrumbs. Add the sugar, currants and mixed spice. Break the egg into a cup or bowl and beat with a fork. Now add the beaten egg and the milk to the ingredients in the bowl and mix together with a wooden spoon to make a stiff dough. Spoon small rough heaps of the mixture fairly well apart on the baking sheet and bake in the oven for about 10 to 15 minutes until golden. Remove from the oven and transfer to a wire rack to cool.

Summer Pudding

So easy to make and so delicious. Use frozen fruits if fresh are not available.

4-6 slices white bread, medium sliced
1-1½ lb (450-700g) soft fruit (a mixture of raspberries, strawberries,
blackcurrants, redcurrants, blackberries etc. as available)
Sugar to taste
Scant ¼ pint (150ml) water

Required: **A saucepan and a 2 pint (1150ml) pudding basin or a round soufflé dish.**

First cut off the crusts from the bread and then cut the slices wedge-shaped so as to fit and line the base and sides of the basin. If including currants or blackberries, put them first into the pan with enough sugar to taste and the water. Bring to the boil and simmer gently until the fruit is almost soft, then add the strawberries and raspberries and cook for a further 3 minutes. Next, fill the basin with the fruit mixture but reserve 2 or 3 tablespoons of juice. Cover the fruit with bread cut to fit the top of the basin and press down. Now put a saucer on top of the basin, place a weight on it and leave in the refrigerator for some hours or overnight. Just before serving, turn out on to a serving dish and use the reserved juice to cover any areas of bread which have been left white. Serve with whipped cream. Serves 4 to 6.

Scotch Pancakes

These are just spoonful of batter fried on a hot pan. Spread with butter and eat warm.

4 oz (110g) self-raising flour
1 oz (25g) caster sugar
1 egg   ¼ pint (150ml) milk

***Required:* A mixing bowl and a heavy frying pan or a griddle.**

First measure the flour and sugar into the bowl and make a hollow well in the centre. Break in the egg, add half of the milk and beat very well with a wooden spoon to produce a thick batter. Now stir in the rest of the milk. Alternatively put all the ingredients into a food processor and blend until smooth. Lightly grease the frying pan and heat up on the stove. Test the temperature by dropping on a small spoonful of batter and if the underside turns brown in under 1 minute the heat is sufficient. Now drop tablespoonsful of batter, well apart, on to the pan. When bubbles appear on the surface, turn the pancake over with a slice or palette knife and cook the other side for ¹/₂ a minute. Wrap the cooked pancakes, as they are made, in a clean tea towel to keep warm and moist before eating. Serve warm spread with butter and jam. Makes about 20 pancakes.

Chicken Hash

A useful meal made from left-over chicken and mashed potato.

12 oz (350g) cooked chicken   12 oz (350g) mashed potato
3 onions, thinly sliced   1 oz (25g) butter   1 tablespoon oil
¼ pint (150ml) chicken stock (use ½ a stock cube)
Salt and pepper   Chopped fresh parsley to garnish

Required: **A mixing bowl and a large frying pan.**

Use left-over mashed potato, if available. If not, then boil sufficient potatoes in salted water and mash. Cut the cooked chicken into tiny pieces and mix with the mashed potato in the bowl. Slice the onions very thinly. Heat the butter and oil in the frying pan and gently fry the onions until softened, but not brown. Pour in and stir sufficient stock (use a stock cube dissolved in hot water) with the chicken/potato mix in the bowl to produce the consistency of thick cream and season very well with salt and pepper. Add this mixture to the onion in the pan, mix all well together and pat flat with a slice. Turn up the heat under the pan and fry until the bottom of the hash is really crisp and brown and well heated right through. Fold over like an omelette, slide on to a hot serving dish and garnish with chopped parsley. If the pan is not big enough, divide the mixture, and fry as two cakes. Serves 4.

METRIC CONVERSIONS

The weights, measures and oven temperatures used in the preceding recipes can be easily converted to their metric equivalents. The conversions listed below are only approximate, having been rounded up or down as may be appropriate.

Weights

Avoirdupois	Metric
1 oz.	just under 30 grams
4 oz. (¼ lb.)	app. 115 grams
8 oz. (½ lb.)	app. 230 grams
1 lb.	454 grams

Liquid Measures

Imperial	Metric
1 tablespoon (liquid only)	20 millilitres
1 fl. oz.	app. 30 millilitres
1 gill (¼ pt.)	app. 145 millilitres
½ pt.	app. 285 millilitres
1 pt.	app. 570 millilitres
1 qt.	app. 1.140 litres

Oven Temperatures

	°Fahrenheit	Gas Mark	°Celsius
Slow	300	2	150
	325	3	170
Moderate	350	4	180
	375	5	190
	400	6	200
Hot	425	7	220
	450	8	230
	475	9	240

Flour as specified in these recipes refers to plain flour unless otherwise described.